WOW

A HANDBOOK FOR LIVING

WOW

A HANDBOOK FOR LIVING

ZEN OHASHI
ZONO KURAZONO

WOW
A Handbook for Living

ISBN: 978-0-9785084-8-7

Authors: Zentaro Ohashi and Keizo Kurazono
Design: Gwyn Kennedy Snider, GKS Creative

Translated by Robert McGuire
Special thanks to Glenn Anderson

Published by One Peace Books

One Peace Books
57 Great Jones Street New York, NY 10012 USA
www.onepeacebooks.com

Printed in Canada

To our friendship ("YUJO" in Japanese).

Zono Kurazono

To Kurumi, my soul is always with you.

Zen Ohashi

A HANDBOOK FOR LIVING

01 What's working for you?
02 Answer in five seconds.
03 Let it out.
04 Tough stuff.
05 How about now?
06 What is the difference between "serious" and "smooth?"
07 Say it with *how.*
08 That makes me sad.
09 What's your idea?
10 What do you need?
11 Everyone has a voice.
12 Rate it.
13 What would your hero say?
14 I'll call you later.
15 I can't help being judgmental.
16 With all you've been through, are you really going to do it?
17 Everyone thinks, "It's not my fault."
18 Don't put up with it anymore.
19 I love you (I hate you).
20 Five stupid things.
21 So you are going to do it...well, when?
22 How are you progressing?
23 Are you looking for the right answer?
24 Questions conquer problems.
25 How do you picture yourself one year from now?
26 I am a little upset with you.
27 Let's try again.
28 I was on fire!
29 It's okay to be selfish.
30 What was it that you didn't say?
31 Are you brave enough to quit?

Wow!

Out of a hundred people there may be only one person who will actually use this book as described below, but for that one person, amazing things will certainly happen.

1. **First, try to do these exercises exactly as they are written.**
   In karate, if you try and rearrange all the moves you've learned, you'll end up eating someone's fist. Similarly, in the beginning, do the exercises in this book as they are written. Once you've mastered them you can go ahead and rearrange them as you see fit.

2. **Try the exercises on your own first. Then, feel free to try them out on other people.**
   What you'll learn is not measured in input, but output. There is a big difference in being able to *understand* something and actually being able to do something. If you find an exercise you like, you should feel free to try it out on someone else.

3. **When things aren't going well, stop looking for the reason why. Instead, think of *how* you could make them go better.**
   Prepare yourself for the best way, timing, partner, and plan. Of course, there will be instances where this won't work.

4. **Whatever you do, don't be in a hurry.**
   Don't try to master this book in three weeks. Those who do will have set a new record. It's not necessary.

This book, like everything else in life, will mean something other than was intended, if while reading it you have preconceptions about what it is you want it to say. If you come at it with your opinions and reactions decided in advance, then it cannot speak to you. If you go through this book with a friend, then perhaps the promises you make to each other will begin to hold a different meaning than before.
If you approach a world that you can't see without holding on to your anxiety, then you'll find things becoming clearer, just like a sunny day.
It may be that results suddenly start soaring, you get what you really want, become more honest with yourself, or find yourself in new situations and building new relationships.
You may still have some doubts, but by the time you've read half of this book I think you'll come to understand what I mean.

I hope that you enjoy this book.

IN THE BEGINNING

Choose one exercise
that stands out to you
and actually do it.

MOOD MAKER

01

What's working for you?

a. Write down what's working for you right now on a sheet of paper.

b. Start a conversation by asking someone, "What's working for you?"

~

If you are in a
good mood,
good things will
happen. It you are
in a bad mood,
bad things will
happen.

How do you get in a
good mood
in under a minute?

"What's working for you?" People rarely ask this question. First, ask someone else this question. Then, let them ask you in return. Talking about what is working and going well for you will significantly improve the mood.

There was a girl whose mother was always complaining, so one day, in the midst of such complaints, the girl suddenly asked,

"So what's working for you?"

In response, her mother suddenly brightened up and said,

"Oh, your grandmother just sent the nicest little gifts."

Once you've asked someone else what's working and going well for them, you can continue by telling them the good things happening in your life.

When discussing a difficult problem with someone, try first to say out loud three things that are going well for each of you. If each person has mentioned three positive things, it is much easier to discuss the problem.

try it

"What's working for you?"

FAST CHESS

02

Answer in five seconds

a.....Think of your biggest problem at the moment and think of a solution within five seconds.

b.....After you have it, take your time to think it over.

c.....Whenever you encounter a problem, provide a solution in five seconds.

If you see someone else
with a problem,
tell him or her to come up
with a solution
in five seconds.

Whenever presented with a tough problem,
it can be very helpful to try
to answer it in five seconds.

Whenever you try to solve a problem in five seconds, you will answer with only your intuition.

Whether the solution can actually
be carried out is not important. Sometimes just knowing
the solution you would choose is the first step.

Oftentimes, this is the best solution.

IT'S ALRIGHT

03

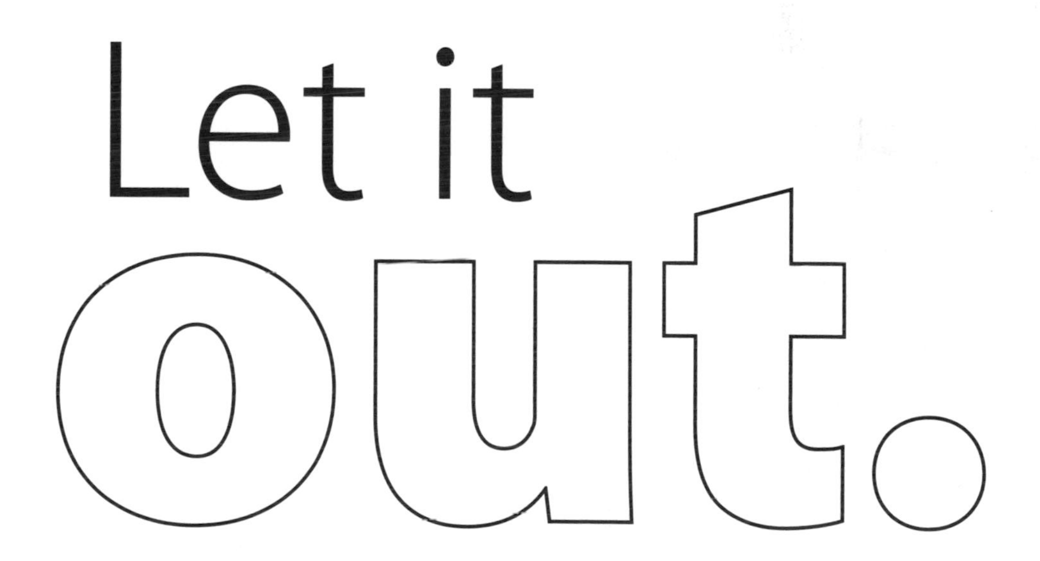

If you feel like crying,
then go ahead and **cry**
—even if you're in front
of other people at the time.

From now on if you want to *cry*, go ahead and **cry**.

Everyone has something in their lives that they just want to seal up in a box. It may be a recent or old failure. It may be a lack of love that they want or need from a parent, child, or spouse. It may even be something that they don't fully understand. There are a lot of things packed away and sealed up in those boxes.

These boxed-up things tend to get in our way whenever we try to take on a new challenge or goal. When we look for the answer to what is holding us back, we often find it difficult to look in those boxes.

Try crying.

By letting out that emotion, you will be able to open the box that you were unable to open before.

If you are able to cry and work through your emotions, you will be able to encourage others to do the same.

NOTHING IS OFF-LIMITS

04

Tough stuff

- ***Write down some problems you face in trying to get to where you want to be.***
- ***After you're done, write down what you weren't able to talk about.***
- ***After you've finished both lists, write down the hard truth related to the problems you wrote down.***
- ***Encourage other people who have problems to do the same.***

An effective way to solve a problem is to attack it at the core. To just jump in and point it out right away takes courage. What's more, if you don't go about it the right way you might find that **you** *are the problem.*

If you try to solve a problem on the surface, it's doubtful that anything good will happen. When a problem occurs, it's difficult to think that you may be mistaken in your diagnosis of it, and everyone is good at fooling him or herself into believing the reasons they've already concocted, even if they are not actually the core of the problem.

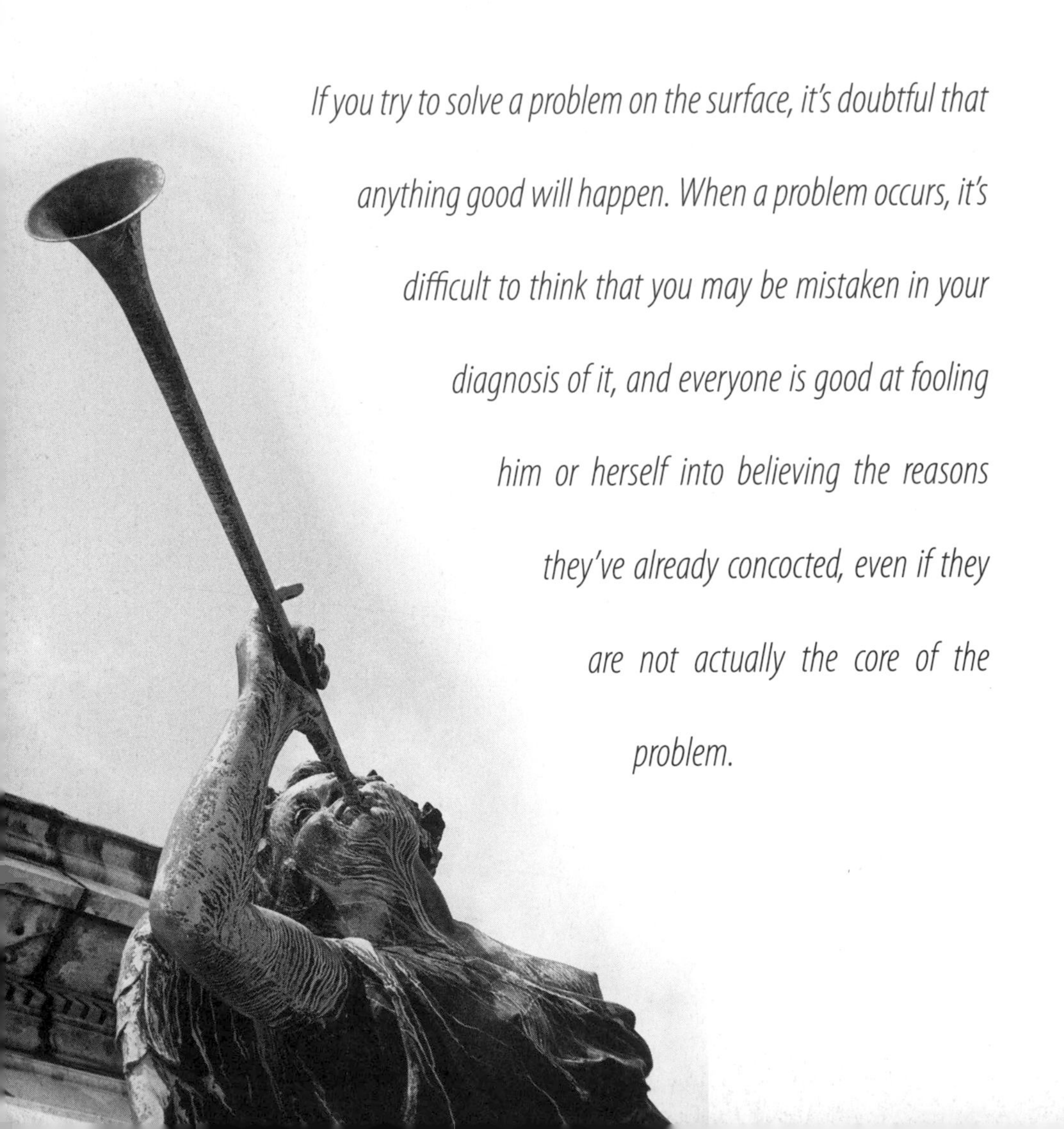

To get at the core of a problem, try asking yourself (or others) the following questions:

What is the hard truth of this problem?

What are some hard truths about you?

CHALLENGE

05

How about **now**?

From the list of things
you've always
wanted to do
but haven't,
choose one
and
do it
in the next twenty-four hours.

Very few people choose to do things that they don't have to do. If you need guts to do something, it's hard to start. You end up saying, "I'll start tomorrow" or "I'll start next week." Before you know it, six months have gone by and then a year.

When that happens, get support. Get a friend to say to you, "Hey, why not do that thing you've been talking about." If you can answer, "Okay, let's do it," make a promise to each other. After you make the promise to get motivated it will feel good to keep that promise.

- How about starting that thing you always wanted to do, **right now**?

- If you're looking at this page and thinking,
- ***"I really want to do that...,"***

start today!

EASY

06

What is the difference between "serious" and "smooth?"

When you feel that you have hit rock bottom, think about the difference between these two words.

When you find yourself struggling over something, ask yourself, what's the difference between serious and smooth?

Let's say there are two kinds of people in the world, smooth people and serious people. But just what are these people like?

A serious person is one who is so concerned with one issue that it overshadows everything else in the person's life. They feel as though they are crushed by a challenge they don't want. They can become obsessed with this type of victim-thinking, and often they secretly pride themselves on their own effort.

A "smooth" person is one who approaches challenges with intention and lightness of thought, someone who doesn't feel sorry for him or herself when something is hard, but instead makes an effort to remain flexible and open to challenge. At the same time, they consider this challenge, along with other issues, to be only aspects of their daily lives, and so their response to the challenge is naturally incorporated into their daily choices.

When you find yourself stretched thin, ask yourself, what is the difference between smooth and serious?

The following is a list of key words to think about when considering these two:

Serious	**Smooth**
heavy, unrelenting, heartless, "it won't work," fear of failure, late, cloudy days	light, willpower, challenges, get it done, responsibility, fast, rainbows

THE WOW METHOD

07

Say it with *how*.

*"**How** am I going to make ____________ happen?"*

When a problem presents itself, the first thing to do is to begin the habit of saying,

"*How* am I going to make __________ happen?"

When a problem occurs, it is only natural to look for the reason why.

"Why was I late?"

"Why don't I have any money?"

"Why did that happen?"

To find the root cause of the problem is important, but if you just ask *why*, chances are that you won't find the real cause. This is because it can be hard to think of yourself as wrong. Instead you can get confused and unable to deal with the fact that maybe *you* are the problem.

At that time it is best to ask:

*"**How** do I stop the problem from happening again?"*

*"**How** will I make sure I'm not late again?"*

*"**How** do I plan to earn more money?"*

How am I going to make ______________ happen?

Now you know how.

TALK ABOUT
STEVIE WONDER

08

That makes me sad.

There may be a situation where you don't like the way someone is behaving. If this is the case, try to tell that person how it makes you feel.

There was a woman who had to get up for work two hours ahead of her husband. She had difficulty getting out of bed right away. Every morning her husband would wake up at the sound of the alarm and roughly push her out of bed growling, "Wake up!" Naturally, she didn't like this very much. How could she react to this?

Two desirable characteristics of a positive outcome:

1. Don't scold or get revenge.

2. The other person changes their behavior of their own accord.

WHENEVER SOMEONE IS OFFENDED, THE TENDENCY IS FIRST TO GET DEFENSIVE AND THEN TO GET REVENGE. BEING SCOLDED OR ATTACKED IN ANY WAY, EVEN WHEN YOU ARE IN THE WRONG, PUTS UP PEOPLE'S DEFENSES AND KEEPS THEM FROM REACHING ANY KIND OF POSITIVE CONCLUSION. FURTHERMORE, BEING TOLD TO "STOP" OR "DO IT THIS WAY" ISN'T FUN FOR ANYONE. IT'S EASY FOR THE OFFENDER TO IGNORE THESE COMMENTS AND CONTINUE THE ACTION UNCHANGED.

THE WOMAN WHO HAD TROUBLE WAKING UP HAD DECIDED TO DO THE FOLLOWING TRUE STORY:

SHE SAID TO HER HUSBAND, "WHEN YOU WAKE ME UP LIKE THAT IT MAKES ME FEEL SAD." SHE WANTED TO SAY MORE, BUT LEFT IT AT THAT AND WALKED OUT THE DOOR FOR WORK. FROM THE NEXT DAY ON HER HUSBAND WAS MUCH NICER.

REAL CONVERSATION

09

What's your idea?

[Before you complain try to begin your sentence with the following words:]

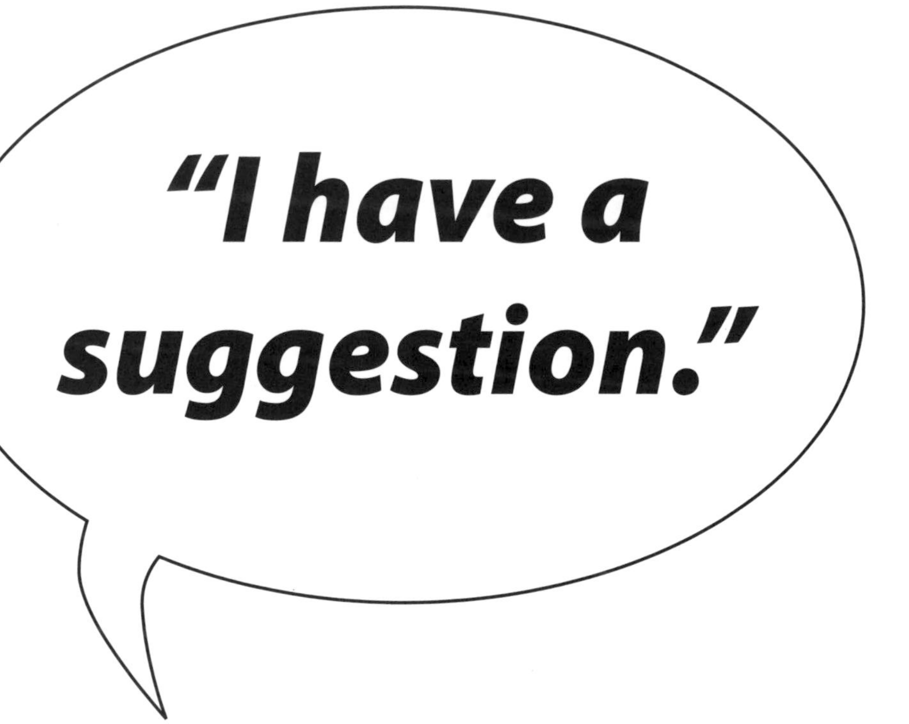

The next time you feel
unsure of yourself or something you are dealing with,
think before you speak.

Instead of complaining, start brainstorming ideas.

When something is bothering you, if you complain or comment on it to someone else, they won't feel like they are being asked for help. For example, if you say something like, "Just laying around on the weekends is a waste of time," then the person you're speaking to will most likely simply agree with the statement or suggestion and that doesn't solve the problem, saying "Yeah, you're right," or "Then why don't you go somewhere?" This tends to just ruin everyone's mood.

Instead, skip the complaint and try to come up with a concrete proposal such as, "I have a plan. Why don't we get a couple of bicycles and go exploring?"

Proposing something new or different often takes ten times more courage than just complaining about it.

However,
it produces
one hundred times
the result.

If the person you propose your idea to doesn't like it and says something like, "Yeah, but it's a bit cold for bicycle riding," you can try asking them for a different proposal.

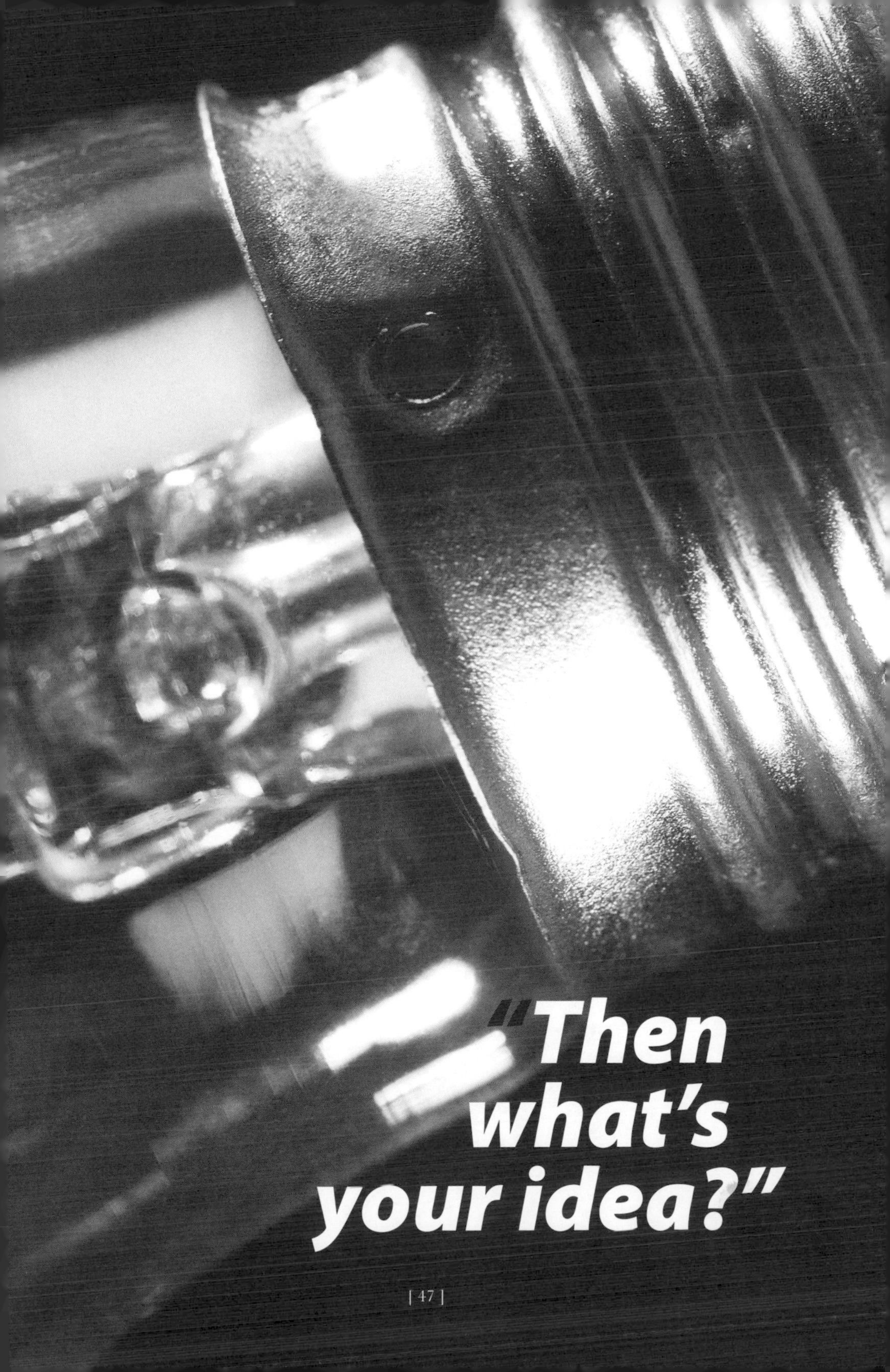

"Then what's your idea?"

REALIZE YOUR ASPIRATIONS

10

What do you need?

The next time you want to tell someone your problem, encourage him or her to ask you the following questions:

1

What state of conditions do you want to create?

2

What do you need?

3

What support do you need to make that happen?

There is a story about a Japanese shogun samurai named Mitsukuni. One day, he was overcome with an idea of implementing social reform among his subjects. However, he was troubled by the difficulty of getting it done.

So, he asked his personal retainer for help.

Mitsu: "I am having some trouble with a certain official."

Retainer: **"What state of conditions would you like to create?"**

Mitsu: "Well, I would like to create a state where the official doesn't cause problems."

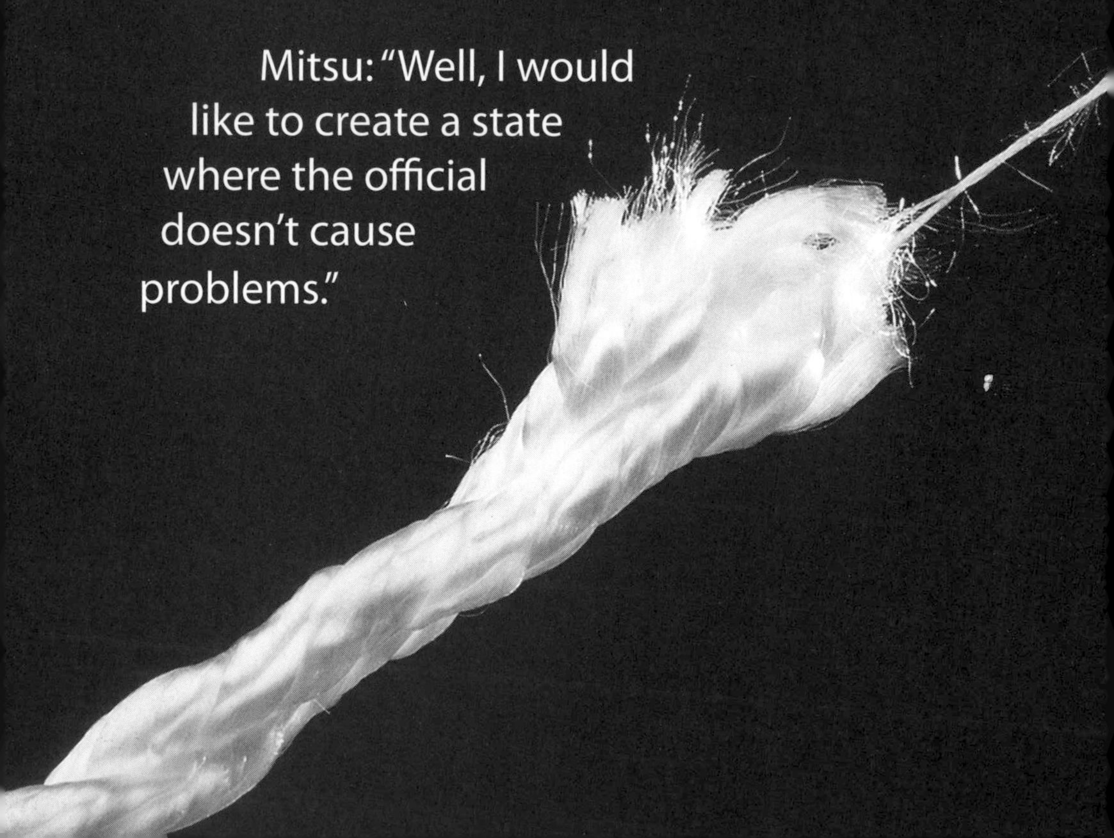

Retainer: **"What do you need to do to make that to happen?"**

Mitsu: "Point out an offense to the official and exercise my authority over him."

Retainer: **"What support do you need to enable that to happen?"**

Mitsu: "First, I need a spy to catch him in the act."

The next time you have a problem like Mitsukuni, try getting your friend to ask you the same questions.

THE WALLFLOWER SPOKE!

11

Everyone has a voice.

Work* TOGETHER *with a partner to write your ideas on paper before you discuss them.

At your next meeting, in order to make things go more smoothly, write down five ideas and discuss them one at a time. Write down your ideas before saying them aloud. Don't allow yourself to be swayed by the other person and propose your ideas with confidence. If you just state them without writing them down, there is a chance some loudmouth will push his or her opinion over yours.

You may think to yourself, "If I say something like that everyone will laugh at me." However, if you don't write up what you want , you may never find the courage to voice your opinion at all. Of course, if you are one of those pushy types, it could be you who is not allowing someone else's opinion to be heard.

For example, this could happen while planning a vacation with your partner. Your partner may say, "We have just got to go somewhere in Asia." But, you had your mind set on Europe and without your idea written down you may never find the courage to speak up.

It is very effective for all parties concerned to write out their ideas on paper during any conversation and discuss them one at a time.

Make sure that *everyone* has a voice, and an opportunity to use it.

ONE DAY YOU ARE AN ELEVEN

12

Rate it.

1 2 3 4 5 6 7 8 9 10 11

If you want to improve your abilities such as

LISTENING

LOVE

ENTHUSIASM

EXPRESSION

rate yourself on a scale of one to ten.

1 2 3 4 5 6 7 8 9 10 11

It may be difficult to measure your ability in things like motivation, love, sensitivity, imagination, concentration, sincerity, acceptance, patience, leadership, self-awareness, decision making, follow-through, ability to listen to others, perseverance, endurance, writing ability, ability to cope with change, and fairness (to name a few).

But if there is ever a time in your life when you feel you want to improve on any of these…

1. Rate the ability on a scale of one to ten, ten being the best you've been able to perform *up to this point in time*, one being the *worst you've ever done*. Do this on a daily basis.

2. To raise your ability just one point, think of what you have to do to improve.

3. ***Try it.***

4. You may find it painful to rate yourself. Remember that good athletes are often motivated by the managers who encourage them. Try to encourage yourself by being generous with your own ratings.

5. Before you know it, there will come a day when you are rating yourself at eleven.

6. If you continue these steps, you won't be surprised by a thirty or 300 point rating.

THE SECRET NINJA TECHNIQUE OF SELF-MULTIPLICATION

13

What would
YOUR HERO
say to you?

WHEN YOU COME TO A TURNING POINT IN YOUR LIFE, TRY ASKING YOURSELF,

"What would my hero say?"

Everyone would like to receive advice from someone they respect and admire. This list could include people like:
Albert Einstein, Wolfgang Amadeus Mozart, Abraham Lincoln, Mohandas Gandhi, William Shakespeare, Pablo Picasso, Marlon Brando, Steven Hawking, John Lennon, George Washington, Mother Teresa, Ernest Hemmingway,
or anyone else you can think of.

Try to imagine what they would say about your situation.

A PROMISE NOT KEPT

14

I'll call you later.

When you ***make a promise***, be sure to set a date and record the outcome.

If there is someone that you aren't extremely eager to make time for, tell them you'd like to meet up for lunch *sometime.*

On the other hand, if there is something you *would* like to do and you don't get it on someone's schedule and make a firm appointment, it most likely will never get done.

If someone promises something to you but does not take the time to make an appointment, it is unlikely that anything will ever happen.

Father: "Hey, Let's go to Disneyland soon."

Daughter: "Cool!"

One month later. . .

Daughter *(looking disappointed):* "Dad, when are we going to Disneyland?"

Ninety percent of anger and sadness result from unfulfilled promises. If you say you are going to do something, follow through and do it.

This will be done by:

(fill in month and day.)

JUDGE NOT...

15

YOU CAN'T LISTEN TO WHAT PEOPLE THINK WITHOUT HAVING AN OPINION OF YOUR OWN.

Whenever you express your opinion try to start with the words,

"I assert..."

or

"My opinion is..."

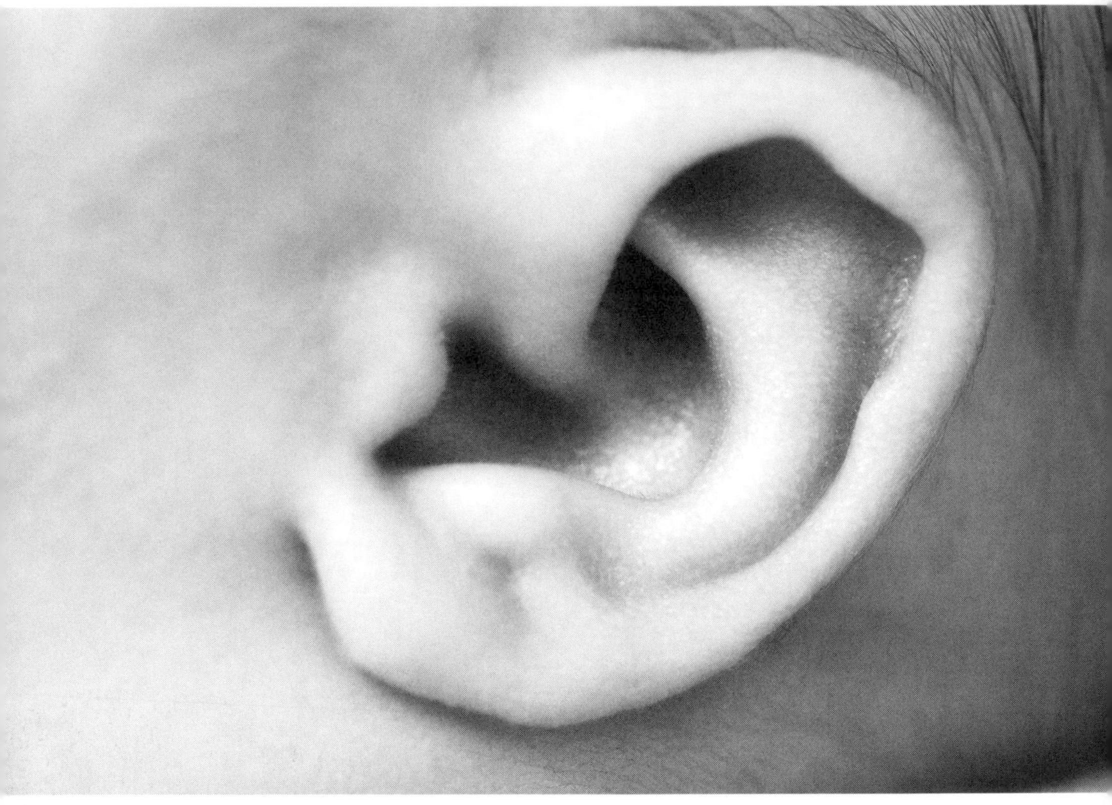

Whenever you're listening to someone else's opinion,
add the words,

"As for your opinion..."

silently to yourself.

Listen to others with sincerity and use "Wind Tunnel Ears."

We all have our own unique set of values based on our experiences from the time we are born up until the present, and it is these values that allow us to determine the worth of what we hear on a day-to-day basis. When we listen to other people talk, we tend to make judgments on what they are saying based on these very values. Because of this, we don't actually listen to a lot of what's being said. This is because we are too busy forming our own opinions.

Try allowing what is being said to pass straight through from your right ear to your left. This type of listening is usually thought of as a bad thing, but if you try it you'll find that you will actually hear a lot more of what the other person is saying.

Then, when you want to respond to someone, try to start with, "As for me..." That way the person to whom you are addressing will think, "I see this is just his opinion, so I don't have to agree with him."

Also when you're listening to someone else's opinion it might help to silently add "in his/her opinion" to yourself. Likewise, whenever expressing a third party's opinion, consider starting with, "This is what he or she thinks..."

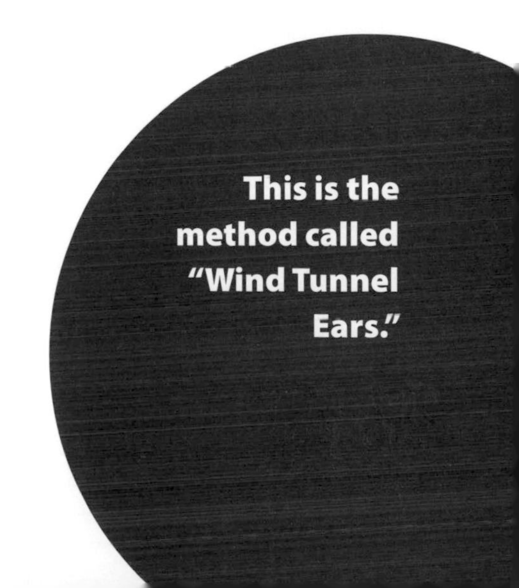

By reforming your listening practices in this manner, you will begin to see what people are saying in a completely different light. You will begin to understand why certain people have certain opinions.

SUPPORTERS

16

WITH ALL THAT YOU HAVE BEEN THROUGH,

are you really going to do it?

1 Once you have a goal, quickly write it down and pin it up on your wall within ten minutes.

2 Ask a friend to call you in one week to see if you have made steps toward your goal.

3 When you find yourself facing an obstacle, get a friend to ask you the questions in this book.

Choose from one of the following options:

PLAN A:

Try to actually carry out one idea found in this book in real life. After a week, you realize that you've made no effort to carry it out.

PLAN B:

Try to actually carry out one idea of this book in real life and follow the advice on the following page.

When you have chosen the idea, write the idea down on paper and put it up in three different places around your home and office.

Ask a friend to call you after one week to see if you have done it.

If you have a support system, you will be reminded of your goals on a daily basis. Encouragement and motivation will replace the fear and uneasiness you used to feel when facing your problems.

It will help you to solve your problems and move forward. Be assured that the person you choose to support you will feel it is an honor rather than a burden to have been asked to do so.

The best time to start this support system is within the next twenty-four hours.

100% + 100% = 100%

17

Everyone thinks,

"IT'S NOT MY FAULT."

Define the difference between...

accountability & responsibility

At a certain famous company, the order of responsibility became clear among top leaders in a power struggle. When one director made a mistake, another director scolded him because it adversely affected his team. In this situation, the second director had clear responsibility over the other because the end result of the mistake affected his team. In such situations, people often end up yelling at each other. Things such as this can also happen at home.

What if there was a project team assigned to the happiness of a child? For example, in a family where one parent is the breadwinner and the other parent takes care of the home, who is in charge of the child's happiness?

Both parents are each 100% in charge.

If the parent in charge of the home becomes sick and is unable to cook, the parent who works has to take over the duties of the sick parent or the child will not eat.

When a problem occurs outside of your normal area of responsibility, it doesn't necessarily mean that you are off the hook.

At home or at work, if everyone takes 100% of the responsibility, it can be very effective in preventing problems.

And if you take 100% of the responsibility and expect others to take on 100% of the responsibility, you will be able to rely on and be relied upon by others.

100% + 100% = 100%

PUTTING UP WITH IT AND ENDURING IT

18

Don't

put up with it *anymore*.

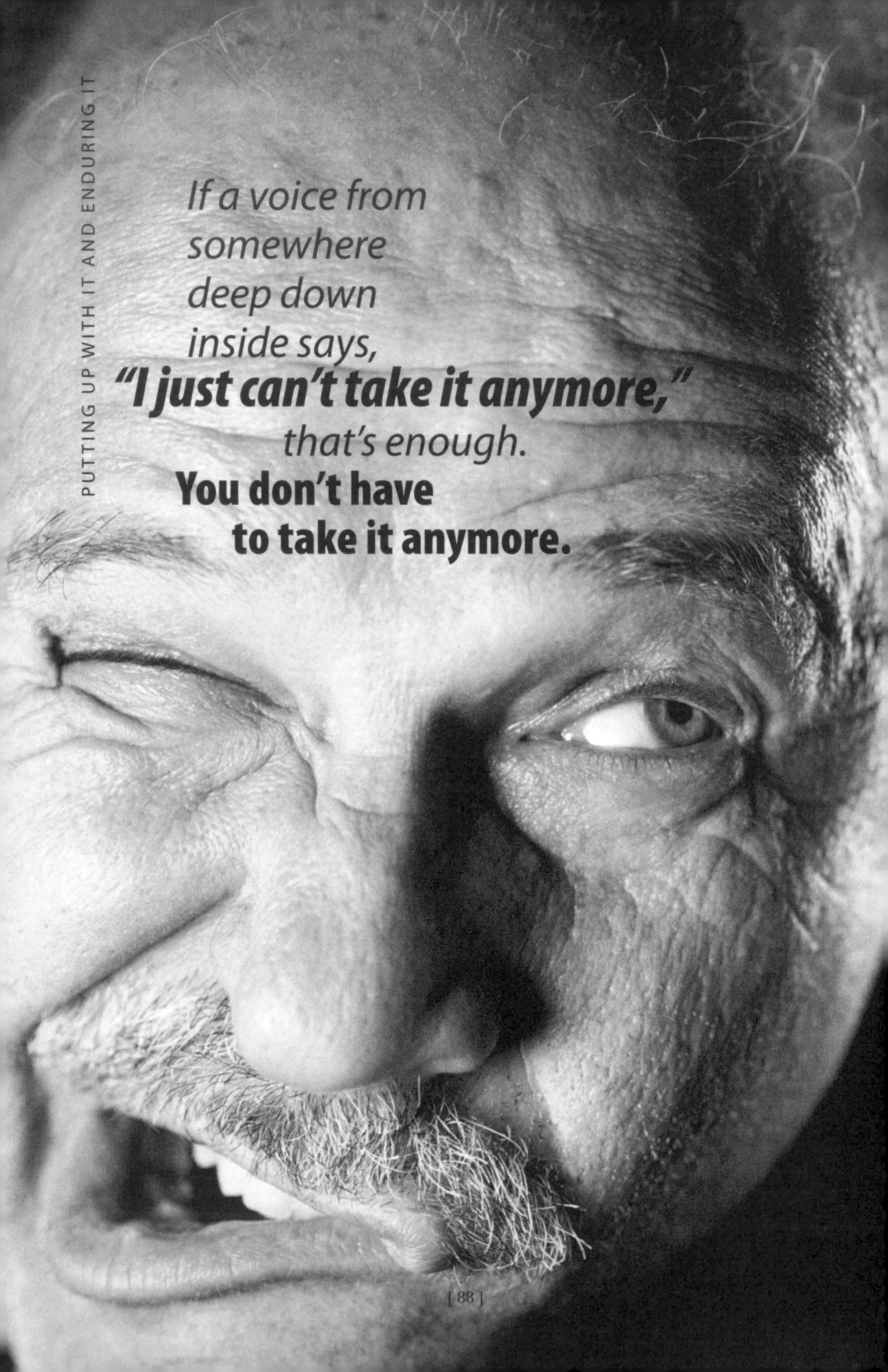

If a voice from somewhere deep down inside says,

"I just can't take it anymore,"

that's enough.

You don't have to take it anymore.

Admitting that you have had enough of something, and then actually quitting that something, takes **courage**. It could mean hurting established relationships. You may lose access to something or lose benefits by stepping away. However, just blindly **"putting up"** with something forever because you think you should, can result in an uninteresting life.

Putting up with something means:

1. To hold back your own desires in order to live with the least amount of resistance.
2. To cave on issues: "This is my life, so I just have to deal with it."
3. That there is no end in sight.

On the flip side, sometimes the situation may require you to endure something in order to reach your goal. This can feel good.

Enduring it means:

1. That in order to protect your values, you choose to accept criticism from others.
2. That you have your own desires.
3. That there is an end to your endurance.

The important thing is to realize when you're "putting up" with something versus enduring something.

I LOVE YOU OR I HATE YOU

19

i love you

(I hate you).

1

When spoken to, try to listen for the unsaid phrases "I love you" or "I hate you."

2

If necessary, tell the person who's talking to you, "I think I heard an "I hate you" in there."

Pay very close attention to what is being said to you during every conversation you have. Try to see if the person is saying, "I love you," or, "I hate you." Listen to the store clerk, the taxi driver, your spouse, your boss, your coworkers, and anyone else.

It's also important to listen very closely to your *own* words the next time you're having a conversation.

When someone is offended, they want revenge, and the most common form of revenge is to show your bad mood to the world. If they are offended by the world then they want revenge on the world. This often comes out during everyday conversation. If a husband has been offended by his wife, he may take it out on someone else. Perhaps he will take it out on a worker at the shop he manages. And when the store clerk has been offended, he might take it out on his customers. If you work in an office and take your anger out on others, it will come back around to you. This can really destroy your mood, as well as the mood of those around you. As you can see, it can become a long chain of anger and resentment.

When someone says, "I hate you," the chain of revenge starts. You may feel that they dislike you and you carry that resentment with you. If you want to break the chain, start by making a conscious effort to cut the chain of revenge. And then, and if possible, with love, ask them what words were silently placed behind their sentence. If you are doing things right, and listen carefully you'll find that there really is a lot of love in the world.

FIVE IN ONE MINUTE

20

Five stupid things.

5

Right after coming up
with a good idea that you have
thought about long and hard,
try coming up with
five stupid ideas
in under a minute.

"Golden tickets in chocolate bars," or "invent a machine for translating dog barks" and others like it are one-time ideas. Chances are that you're going to think most of them aren't any good.

Revolutionary ideas come to us most easily when we create an environment where we are not looking for them. Whenever you are in the process of working out a really good idea, try to come up with five insignificant ones right away. If you are in a group brainstorming, have everyone in the group do the same thing. If you do this you will find that lots of the ideas will, at first, seem really dumb. But, there are bound to be some good ones in there too.

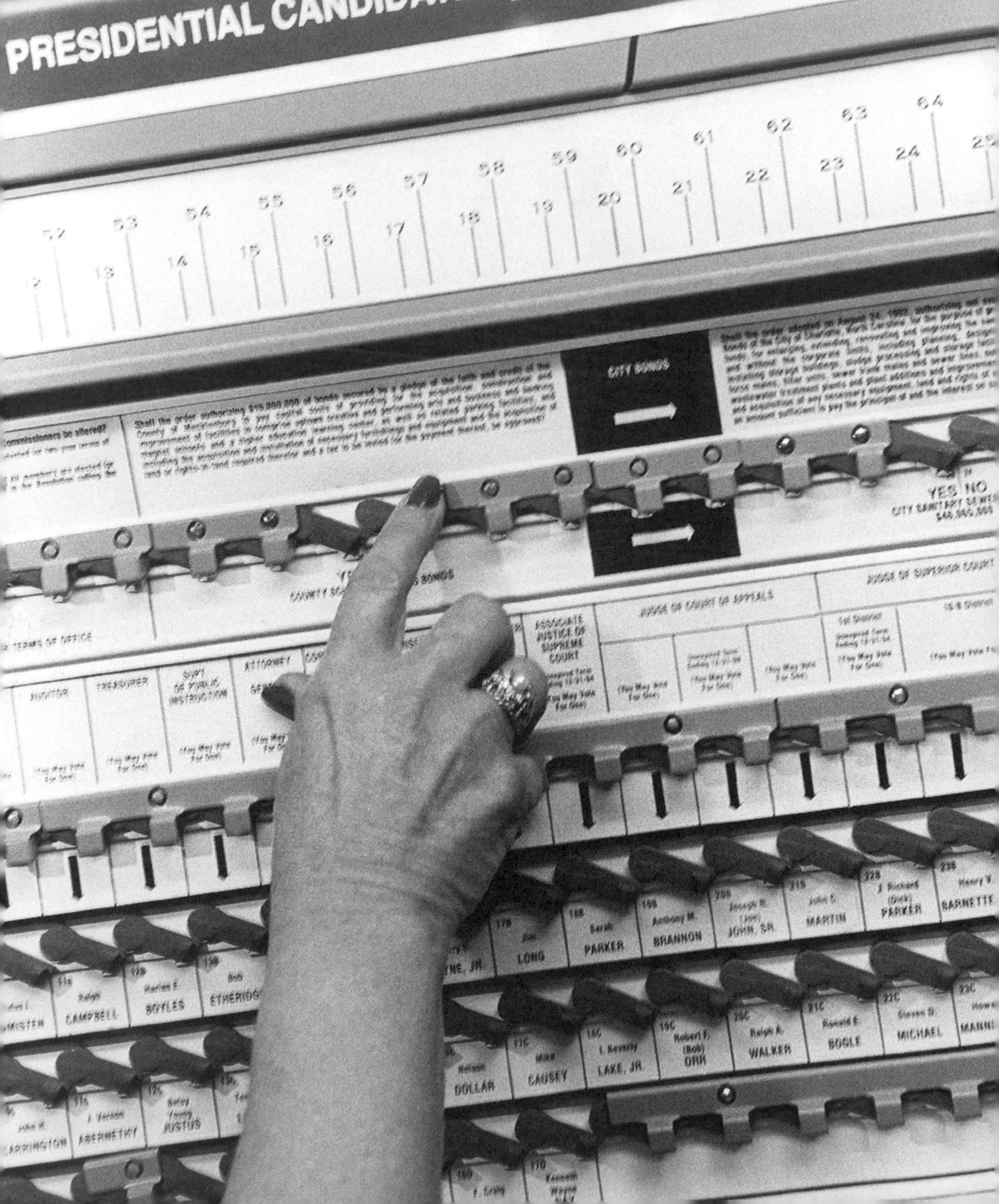

IMPORTANT!
VOTE YOUR PRESIDENTIAL CHOICE
PRESIDENTIAL CANDIDATES ARE NOT ON THE
CITY BONDS
YES NO
AUDITOR
TREASURER
SUPT. OF PUBLIC INSTRUCTION
ASSOCIATE JUSTICE OF SUPREME COURT
JUDGE OF COURT OF APPEALS
JUDGE OF SUPERIOR COURT
Sarah PARKER
LONG
Anthony M. BRANNON
MARTIN
J. Richard (Dick) PARKER
Henry V. BARNETTE
Ralph CAMPBELL
Harlan E. BOYLES
Bob ETHERIDGE
Nelson DOLLAR
Mike CAUSEY
I. Beverly LAKE, JR.
Robert F. (Bob) ORR
Ralph A. WALKER
Ronald E. BOGLE
Steven D. MICHAEL
J. Vernon ABERNETHY
Betsy Young JUSTUS

COMMITMENT

21

SO YOU ARE GOING TO DO IT...

well when?

ONCE YOU HAVE DECIDED TO DO SOMETHING, WRITE DOWN THE DATE BY WHICH YOU ARE GOING TO ACCOMPLISH IT AND WHAT YOU WANT TO HAPPEN AS A RESULT.

WHEN THE TIME COMES TO MAKE A CHOICE, CHOOSE WHAT YOU HAVE COMMITTED TO.

Stick to it.

How will the results differ?

A "I should start on a diet soon" (desire to do something).

B "I will lose ten pounds by July 21st (the exact results and date by which it will be done).

Commitment means sticking to your plan and achieving your goal by the date you set for yourself.

Commitment includes deciding on a date and results.

Everyone has things they want to do, but often they just say they will do them at a later, undefined, date. When you put down an actual date, it increases the chances of actually achieving your goal. When you write down the exact results you're looking for, you can clearly see the path to your goal.

A

"I'll try out this dieting thing. If doesn't work, well, I suppose that's the way it goes."

B

"I won't be able to make my deadline and reach my goal if I keep living the same old way. If I restrict my eating habits in this way, and increase my exercise by this much, I can lose that much weight by my goal date. Now it's very clear!"

Is it easy to stick to a commitment?

No. It's not.

But what could happen if you proceed in this way?

GATEKEEPER

22

How are you progressing?

Whenever you have decided to do something, ask a friend to call or e-mail you and ask,

"How are you progressing?"

In the past, you may have found yourself saying,

"I'm going jogging every morning starting tomorrow."

In three days, you gave up. What if you had someone to jog with you?

If you make plans while you are excited about something, the chances of you sticking to them later are slim. So, once you have a plan, get together with a friend and decide on either a time span (like three months), a time schedule (every Monday), or some type of reward (how about $300?). Have your friend either send you an e-mail or call you to check on the status of your progress. Have your friend call on a specific date to check in and ask you ***"so how is it going?"*** Respond with what has happened since the last check in, as well as what you plan to do by the next check in. Mention again the dates by which you intend to accomplish your goals. If you decide to do this, the chance of meeting your goals will skyrocket.

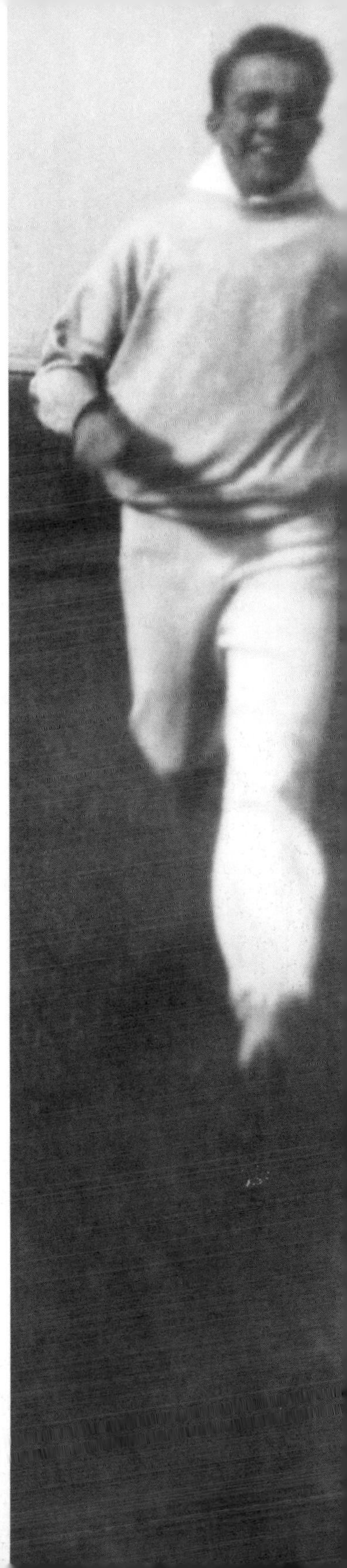

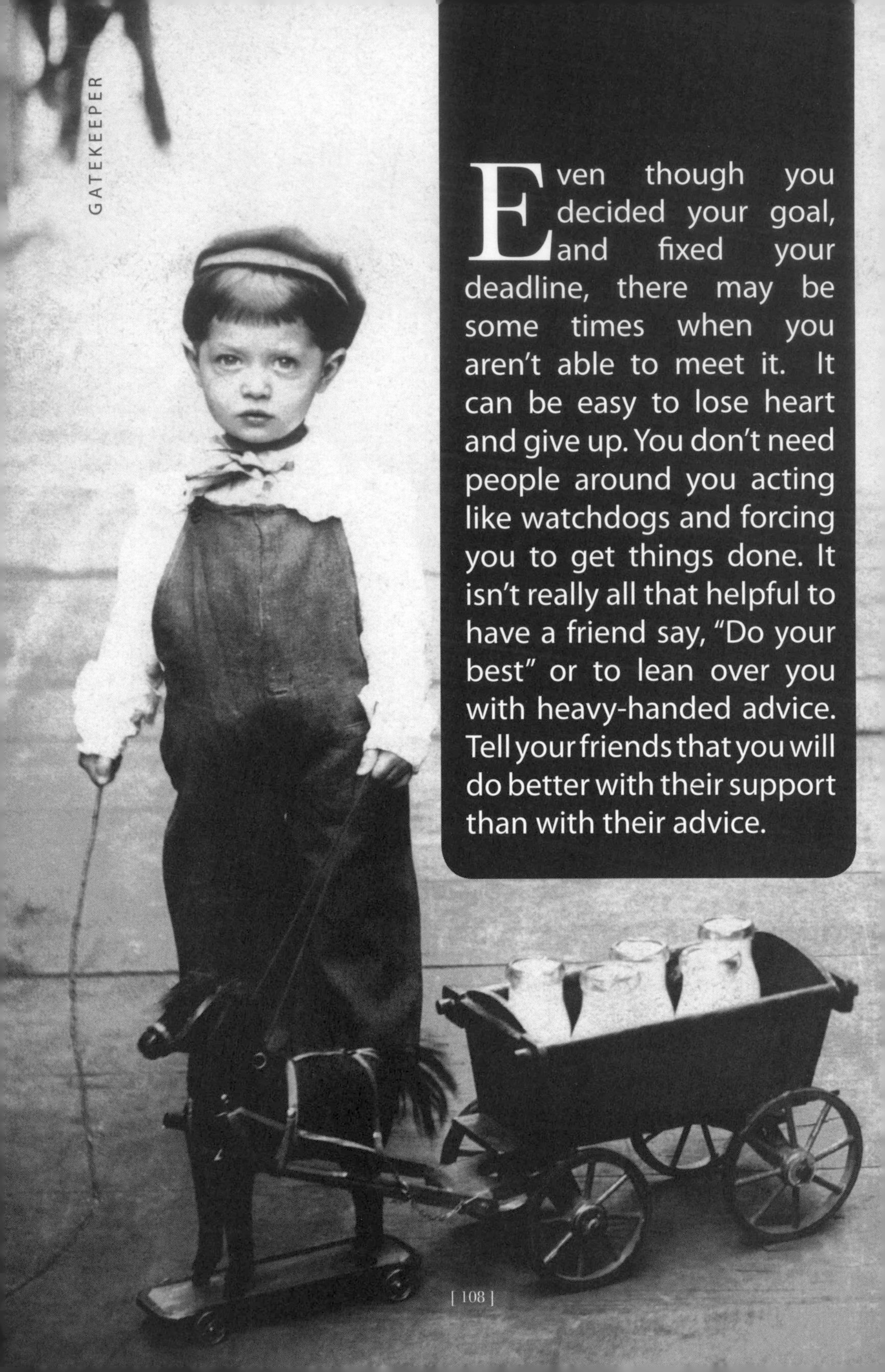

Even though you decided your goal, and fixed your deadline, there may be some times when you aren't able to meet it. It can be easy to lose heart and give up. You don't need people around you acting like watchdogs and forcing you to get things done. It isn't really all that helpful to have a friend say, "Do your best" or to lean over you with heavy-handed advice. Tell your friends that you will do better with their support than with their advice.

THERE IS NO ONE AND ONLY ANSWER

23

Are you looking for the right answer?

Try to live for a month with the premise that there is no one and only right answer.

If it works,
try another month
(Continue repeating indefinitely.)

There is a huge difference in results between a person looking for the "right" answer and a person looking for an answer that "works."

Everyone wants to find the right answer and thinks that it will solve their problems. When looking for that right answer, they are limited to outside influence and restrictions set up by society and the world around them. They are looking for the flawless answer. To find this answer it will take too much time. It may take forever.

By not thinking whether an answer is right or wrong, but instead thinking whether an answer works for you, you will have more freedom and increase your options. For one month, forget about what "right" means. Think about the conditions around you and choose what works. Even while looking at other methods, you won't be swayed.

It is hard to understand how effective this is until you actually try it out. *You have to choose what you feel is a good answer.* If that doesn't work then you can always try something else.

SHOWING SIGNS OF WEAKNESS

24

Questions conquer problems.

When you suddenly realize, "I'm worrying about something," have a friend ask you the questions put forth in this book.

In life, you are sure to encounter all kinds of problems.

Oftentimes, you know the specific thing that you are worried about. It could be relationship problems, your job, or something with your kids. But, the right solution never seems to present itself.

No one *wants* to think about a problem they don't *have* to think about. But, if you find someone to ask you specific questions that are designed to solve problems, you can change your serious and unclear worries into solutions. Find a friend who will ask you the questions in this book (questions like those on page 51). If you are worried about something, pick up the phone. Or, better yet, meet up with your friend. It is better to have a real person ask you each question rather than reading and answering them yourself. This way you will have the tendency to face the real problem and answer with real solutions.

Useful questions can conquer your problems!

FUTURE

25

How do you picture yourself one year from now?

Read the following questions or have someone ask them of you.

1 Where do you see yourself one year from now?

2 Where do you see yourself three years from now?

3 What obstacles will you face before you get there?

4 What would help you get there? Who could help you face those obstacles and obtain your goals?

- You don't know how to deal with the things happening around you.
- You will continue doing what you've been doing for the past two or three years, expect it will stay the same for the next ten, and that doesn't sound too appealing.
- You have started thinking about changing jobs.
- You worry a lot.
- You find it easier and easier to explain why you are unable to do the things you really want to do.
- You are planning on buying something really expensive.

If you fit any of those descriptions, have a friend ask you the following questions.

1. Where do you see yourself one year from now?
2. Where do you see yourself three years from now?
3. What obstacles will you face before you get there?
4. What would help you get there? Who could help you face those obstacles and obtain your goals?

*For question number four, the answer could be someone you don't know. For example, maybe you want to be a Cessna pilot. Your answer might be, "Someone to teach me how to fly a Cessna. "Well, the next question would be, "How are you going to find that person?"

LARRY BIRD

26

I am a

upset with you.

Whenever you are annoyed with something or someone, tell that person directly and calmly,

"That really bothers me."

If you think the person you are talking to is annoyed with you, ask

"Are you angry with me somehow?"

LARRY BIRD

If you are annoyed by something or if something is rubbing you the wrong way, calmly and, if possible, with love, let them know. If you don't, then the problem will only get bigger and you will hold it in until you explode. When something is bothering you, put it on the table. This way you can avoid prolonging any problems that might result from holding it in. When you decide on this approach, be sure to tell your boss, your friends, spouse, coworkers, and anyone else. This way you can all be on the same page from the start, and no one will be unnecessarily hurt.

Don't always be the one to say *'yes'* ***and*** *'I'm sorry'* ***when you don't need or want to.***

When someone does something you don't like, let them know!

27

Let's try again.

again.

again.

again.

EVEN IF A PROMISE HAS BEEN BROKEN,

AS LONG AS THE PERSON CONCERNED

MADE AN HONEST EFFORT,

forgive them.

There are people...

...who have the best intentions and do their best to carry out their job, but still aren't able to produce the results they promised. If you blame a person for failure, the next time they promise you something, it will only be for the results that they are certain they can achieve.

If someone promises
only to the extent they know
they can perform,
then there is no room
for new challenges.

If you want to ***inspire confidence*** and a willingness to take risks, just let it go one time if results were not achieved. If you can do this, then you can ***forgive yourself*** for results not achieved and inspire confidence and a willingness to ***take risks*** in yourself as well. There may be nothing more difficult in the world than forgiving yourself. But if you can, you will find increased ***power and vigor*** in the next challenge you undertake.

PULLING OUT THE UMBRELLA AFTER THE RAIN HAS STOPPED

28

I was on ***fire!***

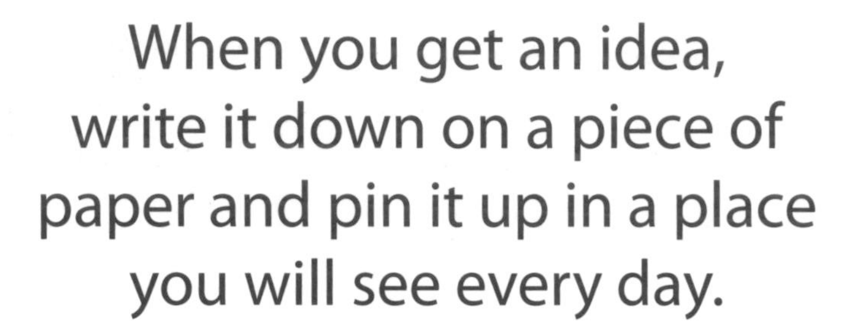

When you get an idea, write it down on a piece of paper and pin it up in a place you will see every day.

Find something that symbolizes your goal and hang that up as well.

Either today or tomorrow, set aside an hour for yourself and take the following action:

Write down a goal on a piece of paper and/or find something that symbolizes your goal and put it in a place where you will be able to see it all the time.

PULLING OUT THE UMBRELLA AFTER THE RAIN HAS STOPPED

People often forget their goals. And the things that would help you realize your goals are not limited to what you wanted to do at the time. ***When you come up with a goal, you are in a state of excitement and full of willpower, dreams, and hope.*** *If you write down your goal at the time you set it and then hang it up, not only will you remember the goal itself, but you will remember the mood you were in when you set the goal. This is most effective if you paste the idea up within five minutes of it coming to you. Hanging your goal on the wall will act like a magic charm, granting you the ability to pursue it on a daily basis.*

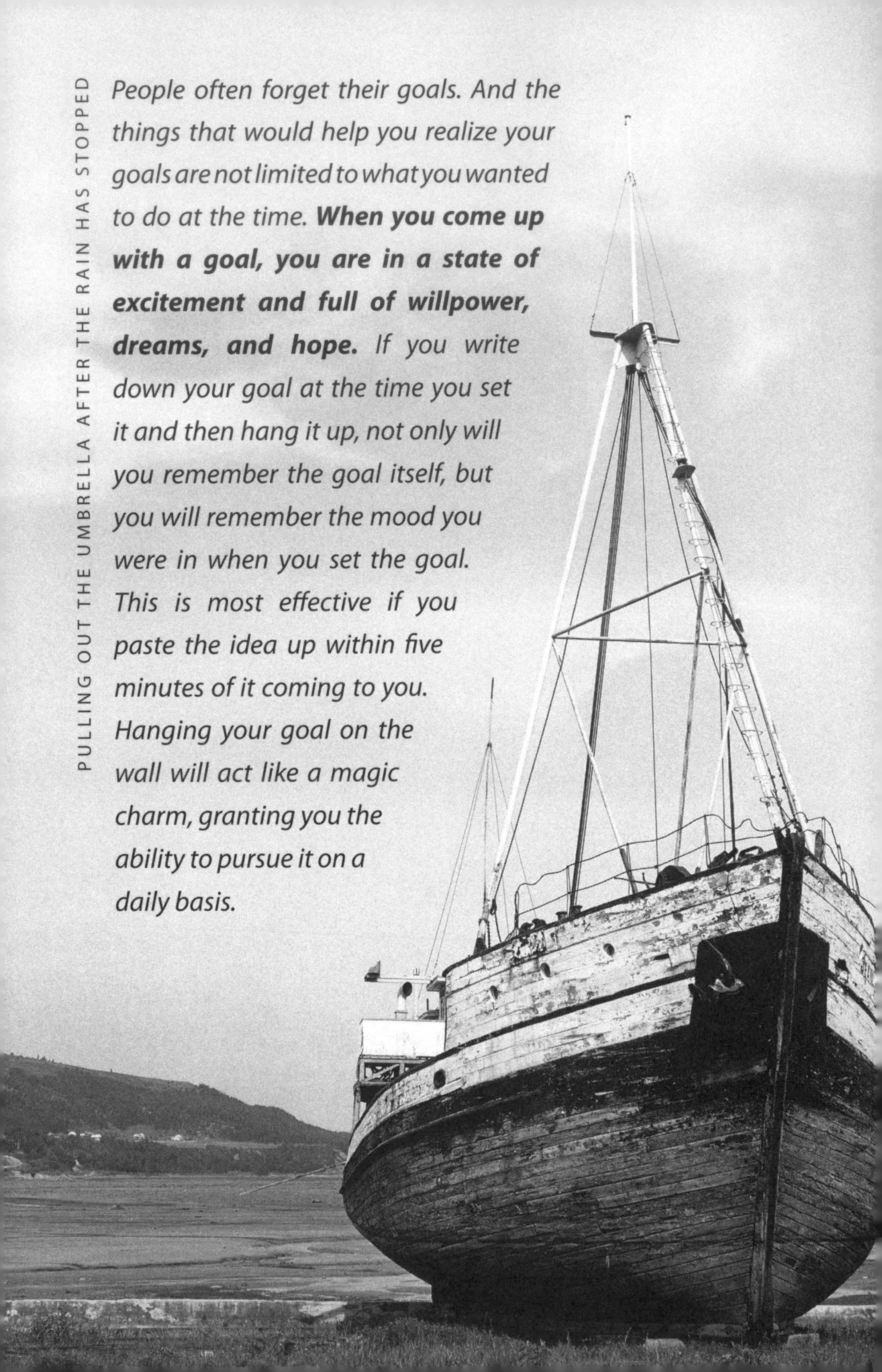

EGOIST

29

It's okay to be selfish.

If you feel really lost,

THINK ABOUT THE PROS
AND CONS OF BEING SELFISH.

In the next week, choose one selfish action and do it. Give in to your ego and your desires and make selfish choices. If you are too conscious of the world around you and what people think, you will have the tendency to forget to do this. In the next week, choose one selfish thing and carry it out. Ask yourself....

"What do I have to do to carry out my desire?"

Merits of not being selfish:

- You won't be branded a troublemaker.
- You don't have to do anything to get what you want.
- You don't have to look for a way to live beyond that which society provides for you.

Merits of being selfish:

- New possibilities and freedoms will present themselves.
- Your life will take on the shade you like.
- You can meet selfish friends and lovers.

THINGS THAT ARE NOT SAID

30

What was it that you didn't say?

The next time you are in a restaurant, try to listen closely to what the couple next to you is talking about. Try to hear what goes unsaid.

The next time you and a friend are in a restaurant, try eavesdropping on the conversation of a couple sitting nearby. Don't necessarily listen to what is *said,* but instead try to hear what goes *unsaid*. When the couple leaves, try saying to your friend the things that the couple actually wanted to say.

Man: "You look tired."

(In other words: Even though you're with me, you look bored.)

Woman: "Yeah…I have been really busy lately."

(In other words: I am really sick of dating this loser.)

If you try this, you will discover the real tone of conversation. After practicing at the restaurant, you will be able to begin to hear the real tone of conversations in all areas of your life. You will become sensitive to what others actually want to communicate aside from what they are saying.

The things that go unsaid are often "Hard truths" (page 19) and will provide a hint to solving a problem. You will find out that speaking with hidden messages doesn't help and you may even start talking more honestly to others.

WITH JUST A GLANCE, IT MAY LOOK IRRESPONSIBLE

31

Are you ***brave enough*** *to quit?*

When you form a goal,
know that you are...

free to change it,

give up on it,

or hold on to it.

It's up to you.

They're all okay.

How do you know whether to continue pursuing your goal or give it up?

WHEN YOU THINK ABOUT GIVING UP ON A GOAL, YOU MAY FIND THAT YOU INSTINCTIVELY RESIST EVEN THE THOUGHT. AFTER SOME TIME HAS PASSED AND YOU FEEL THAT, EVEN IF THE ORIGINAL PREMISE FOR YOUR GOAL WAS WRONG AND YOU CAN SEE NO CHANCE FOR SUCCESS, YOU MIGHT STILL DECIDE THAT YOU DON'T WANT TO GIVE UP. YOU MAY STUBBORNLY CLING TO YOUR GOAL, RESOLVED TO NOT GIVE UP, AND BECOME A "VICTIM" OF THE GOAL. IN THIS CASE, YOU MAY FIND MANY RATHER UNFORTUNATE THINGS BEGIN TO HAPPEN AROUND YOU. PERHAPS WHEN YOU SET THE GOAL, YOU DIDN'T THINK ABOUT WHETHER IT WAS GOOD FOR YOU OR NOT.

YOU CAN CHANGE YOUR GOAL, YOU CAN GIVE UP, OR YOU CAN CONTINUE. IF, FOR SOME REASON, YOU HAVE SOME DOUBTS ALONG THE WAY, MAKE SURE YOU ASK YOURSELF, "WOULD I STILL HAVE MADE THIS GOAL TODAY?" IF THE ANSWER IS NO, EMBRACE THE CHALLENGE OF GIVING IT UP OR CHANGING IT. ACCEPT THE NEW FEELINGS AND IDEAS YOU HAVE ALONG THE WAY. IF YOU EMBRACE THE FREEDOM YOU HAVE TO CHANGE YOUR GOALS TO SUIT YOUR NEEDS, YOU CAN BE LIBERATED FROM BEING "VICTIMIZED" BY THEM.

afterword

About a year before this book was written, there was something that had me a little worried. I had an acquaintance interested in putting my methods into practice at a certain company. I was asked to create some materials for the director. Though I had agreed to deliver the documents within two weeks, I just didn't feel as though I could write them. And no matter what I wrote, it just didn't seem any good.

Worrying about it wasn't getting me anywhere. I had to ask a friend familiar with my program to call me up to ask me the questions on page 51. In response to the question, "What support do you need to allow it to happen," I reached out to a friend. I asked a member of my band, a magazine editor named Zono, who knew of my method, to prepare the presentation materials for me.

I called him up and told him, "I'll talk about my method and you write it down for the clients. I'll pay you 100 dollars." He gave his consent and came over right away. I explained my method in about fifteen minutes. At this point, my friend stood up and slapped a two by two and a half foot giant Post-it on the wall. It read:

> ***Standard*** *($100): simply transcribe exactly what's said directly on to paper*
>
> ***Premium*** *($500): take notes on what's said and prepare materials*
>
> ***Executive*** *($1,000): take notes on what's said and prepare materials that will not only be presentable and clear, but passionate and interesting*

After giving me the options, he asked me to choose one. After deliberating for about fifteen seconds, I chose the Executive option. The project lasted a year and the result was this book. Throughout its production, there were many times I would become upset and say, "Let's just give up." But, he wouldn't. I have to say thank you to Zono for putting his heart and soul into it and trudging on.

Thanks also to Director Iwata of iSi Dentsu, to Gen Taguchi for his good questions, and to my clients that take care of me. Thanks to my family for their wonderful support, to Lisa and Howard Goldman, to director Hirata of the Fusou Company, who backed my plans wholeheartedly and with whose help the miracle of the book came alive.

Next, I have to thank all the people who used my method and sent all your encouraging messages. They give me courage everyday. I hope that my daughter, who is in elementary school, will be able to live a bigger life with a method like mine. I wrote this book for all you readers out there. If you can use my method to make things happen in your life, I am happy.

Zen Ohashi

Who do you think was the first person to buy a copy of this book? It was a young woman who worked at Kinko's. Once Zen and I had finished writing the book we were so happy that we went out, bought some high quality paper, and printed it out.

We printed out one method of advice per page and thought it was wonderful. We took it around to show our friends and brag. One day, Zen came to me and said, "Let's bind it and sell it."

To produce the books was costly, so we sold it for eighteen dollars a copy. People who bought it might recommend it to a friend, so we included our e-mail address and a message so that if anyone wanted to purchase a copy, they would know where to direct their inquiries.

I printed twenty copies at home and gave them to Zen to take to Kinko's to have ring bound.

That evening I got an e-mail request to buy a copy. It was from the young woman who worked at Kinko's. She gets twenty or thirty projects to be bound a day. I wouldn't have thought she would spend time actually looking through the content. There was something that attracted her to our message and before she knew it, she became the first person to purchase our book.

It was then that I became convinced to put this book out into the world. I thought if a woman at Kinko's who puts together short books like these all day wants to buy our book, so would other people. We sent Ms. Hirata at Fusou Company a copy and her response came almost frighteningly fast. They wanted to publish it. Ikari, their editor, with his magnificent sense, cleaned it up and turned out something professional. To those two people who turned our dream into a reality, I thank you.

Zen had envisioned the idea of this book and both of us were firmly against putting in anything that wasn't proven. In other words, the methods in this book have been used and proven to produce results in our own lives. There is nothing in this book that has not been proven effective. I want to thank Zen for having the power to realize this in this book. And I want to thank my wife for her daily encouragement.

Most of all, I want to thank all the readers out there who bought this book and used these methods in their lives. From the bottom of my heart, thank you.

Zono Kurazono